Amazing
Breakfast Sandwich Recipes

51 Quick & Easy, Delicious Breakfast Sandwich Recipes for the Busy Person Using a Breakfast Sandwich Maker

Table of Contents

Introduction

*"When you wake up in the morning, Pooh,"
said Piglet at last, "what's the first thing you
say to yourself?"*

*"What's for breakfast?" said Pooh. "What do
you say, Piglet?"*

*"I say, I wonder what's going to happen
exciting today?" said Piglet.*

*Pooh nodded thoughtfully. "It's the same
thing," he said.*

- A.A. Milne

Our world is full of people who are
constantly on the go. Work, school,
parenting and a list of numerous other
activities keep us hopping. Because of this,
breakfast is too frequently passed by.

Eating a meal first thing in the day does many things for the body. Besides giving you a feeling of satisfaction, eating breakfast has been proven in studies to jump start your metabolism, help balance your blood sugar and help you be healthier overall. Many studies show people who eat breakfast are slimmer and happier, especially if the food consumed is of high quality.

The breakfast sandwich recipes in this book are the perfect solution to busy days and nutritious food. They're quick and easy, full of the nutrients your body can use, and are delicious to boot! These meals will help keep your body working well through the morning.

Sandwich makers are the perfect tool to create easy breakfast sandwiches. They provide you with an amazing meal that's perfect whether you're running out the door, or want to eat at home. No more stopping at a greasy fast food place to grab your breakfast!

Some tips to help make your sandwich maker work optimally:

Don't Overfill:

Make sure to only put the recommended amount of ingredients in the sandwich maker so as to avoid a mess.

Preheat:

Your sandwich will cook more evenly if you let the machine preheat. It only takes a few minutes.

Spray Lightly:

Sandwich makers have a non-stick surface; however it is helpful to keep in mind that you may need to lightly spray the unit with non-stick cooking spray to ensure your sandwich doesn't stick.

Easy Clean-up:

Sandwich makers are easy to clean using a damp kitchen towel and many parts are dishwasher safe.

How to Slide the Egg Plate Out:

After the sandwich has cooked, gently slide the egg plate out by turning the handle clockwise, and then remove the sandwich.

The Recipes

The Ham & Cheese

1 English muffin, split

Grainy mustard

1 slice honey spiral ham

1 slice cheddar cheese

1 egg

Red Hot sauce

Spread some grainy mustard on both halves of English muffin. Place one half, mustard side up into the bottom ring of breakfast sandwich maker. Place ham and cheddar cheese on top.

Lower the cooking plate and top ring; crack an egg into the egg plate and pierce to break the yolk. Sprinkle a few drops of Red Hot sauce on the egg and top with other muffin half.

Close the cover and cook for 4 to 5 minutes or until egg is cooked through. Gently slide the egg plate out and remove sandwich with a rubber spatula.

Prep time: 4 minutes   Serves: 1

Southwest Quesadilla

2 small corn tortillas

3 slices avocado

Sea salt and pepper

1 slice tomato

1 slice Monterey Jack cheese

Fresh chopped cilantro

1 egg

Place one corn tortilla in the bottom of sandwich maker. Place avocado on top and sprinkle with sea salt and pepper. Then add tomato, Monterey Jack cheese and sprinkle with cilantro.

Lower the cooking plate and top ring; crack an egg into the egg plate and pierce to break the yolk. Place other corn tortilla on top and close the lid.

Cook for 3 to 4 minutes or until egg is cooked through. Gently slide the egg plate out and remove quesadilla with a rubber spatula. Slice in half and serve.

Prep time: 4 minutes   Serves: 1

Maple Bacon Waffle Sandwich

2 small round waffles (store bought or homemade)

Maple syrup

2 strips maple bacon

1 slice cheddar cheese

1 egg

1 Tbsp. milk

Sea salt and pepper

Place one waffle in the bottom of sandwich maker. Drizzle some maple syrup on top, then the maple bacon and cheddar cheese.

Lower the cooking plate and top ring. In a small bowl, whisk together egg, milk, sea salt and pepper; pour into egg plate. Top with other waffle.

Close the cover and cook for 4 to 5 minutes or until egg is cooked through and cheese is melted. Slide the egg plate out and remove sandwich with a rubber spatula. Cut in half.

Prep time: 4 minutes   Serves: 1

Pesto Italian Bagel

1 bagel, split

1 Tbsp. store bought pesto

1 slice ham

4 round slices pepperoni

1 slice tomato

1 slice provolone cheese

1 egg

Spread pesto on both halves of bagel. Place one half, pesto side up into the bottom ring of breakfast sandwich maker. Place ham, pepperoni, tomato and provolone cheese on top.

Lower the cooking plate and top ring; crack an egg into the egg plate and pierce to break the yolk. Top with other bagel half.

Close the cover and cook for 4 to 5 minutes or until egg is cooked through. Gently slide

the egg plate out and remove sandwich with
a rubber spatula.

Prep time: 5 minutes   Serves: 1

Pancake, Sausage & Egg Sandwich

2 small store bought or homemade pancakes

Butter

1 precooked sausage patty

1 slice cheddar cheese

1 egg

Butter each pancake and place one, butter side up, into the bottom ring of breakfast sandwich maker. Place sausage patty and cheddar cheese on top.

Lower the cooking plate and top ring; crack an egg into the egg plate and pierce to break the yolk; top with other buttered pancake.

Close the cover and cook for 4 to 5 minutes or until egg is cooked through. Gently slide the egg plate out and remove sandwich with

a rubber spatula.

Prep time: 3 minutes   Serves: 1

Cheddar-Apple Smoked Bacon Sandwich

1 English muffin, split

1 tsp. grainy mustard

2 slices smoked bacon

3 thin apple slices

1 slice cheddar cheese

1 egg

Spread the mustard on one half of the English muffin. Place muffin, mustard side up, into the bottom ring of breakfast sandwich maker. Place smoked bacon, apple slices and cheddar cheese on top.

Lower the cooking plate and top ring; crack an egg into the egg plate and pierce to break the yolk; top with other English muffin half.

Close the cover and cook for 4 to 5 minutes

or until egg is cooked through. Gently slide the egg plate out and remove sandwich with a rubber spatula.

Prep time: 4 minutes   **Serves: 1**

Almond Butter & Honey Biscuit

1 store bought or homemade biscuit, split

1 Tbsp. almond butter

1 – 2 tsp. honey

Dash of cinnamon

Spread the almond butter on half of the biscuit and then drizzle honey on top. Place biscuit, almond butter side up, into the bottom ring of breakfast sandwich maker. Sprinkle with cinnamon.

Lower the cooking plate and top ring and top with other biscuit half. Close the cover and cook for 3 to 4 minutes or until biscuit is warmed through. Remove sandwich with a rubber spatula.

Prep time: 3 minutes   Serves: 1

Spicy Cream Cheese Raspberry Croissant

1 small croissant, sliced in half

1 – 2 Tbsp. cream cheese

1 – 2 Tbsp. raspberry jam

1 small jalapeño, seeded and sliced in thin rings

Spread cream cheese and raspberry jam on bottom half of croissant. Place in the bottom of breakfast sandwich maker. Sprinkle with a few jalapeño rings (to taste).

Lower cooking plate and top ring. Place other half of croissant on top and close the sandwich maker lid. Cook for 2 – 3 minutes or until the cream cheese is melted and sandwich is warm. Carefully remove from sandwich maker and enjoy!

Prep time: 3 minutes   Serves: 1

19

Spinach Havarti Sandwich

1 English muffin

2 tsp. mayonnaise

$1/2$ tsp. yellow mustard

A few baby spinach leaves

1 slice Havarti cheese

1 egg

Sea salt and pepper

Spread the mayonnaise and mustard on both halves of English muffin. Place one half, mayo/mustard side up into the bottom ring of breakfast sandwich maker. Place baby spinach leaves and Havarti cheese on top.

Lower the cooking plate and top ring; crack an egg into the egg plate and pierce to break the yolk. Sprinkle some sea salt and pepper on the egg and top with other muffin half.

Close the cover and cook for 4 to 5 minutes or until egg is cooked through. Gently slide the egg plate out and remove sandwich with a rubber spatula.

Prep time: 4 minutes   Serves: 1

Chocolate Banana Croissant

1 small croissant, sliced in half

1 Tbsp. chocolate hazelnut spread

3 – 4 slices of banana

Shredded coconut

Spread chocolate hazelnut spread on bottom half of croissant. Place in the bottom of breakfast sandwich maker. Place banana slices on top. Sprinkle with some shredded coconut.

Lower cooking plate and top ring. Place other half of croissant on top and close the sandwich maker lid. Cook for 2 – 3 minutes or until the croissant is warmed through. Carefully remove from sandwich maker. Enjoy immediately.

Prep time: 3 minutes   Serves: 1

Peanut Butter Magic

1 cinnamon and raisin bagel, split

1 Tbsp. peanut butter

2 tsp. honey

Banana slices

Apple slices

Dash of cinnamon

Spread peanut butter on both bagel halves. Place one half into the bottom ring of breakfast sandwich maker, peanut butter side up. Drizzle honey and place banana and apple slices on top. Sprinkle with cinnamon.

Lower cooking plate and top ring; top with other bagel half. Close the cover and cook for 3 to 4 minutes or until sandwich is warmed. Remove from sandwich maker and enjoy!

Prep time: 4 minutes   Serves: 1

Canadian Bacon & Provolone Bagel

1 bagel, split

1 slice Canadian bacon

1 slice tomato

1 slice provolone cheese

1 egg

Dash of Tabasco sauce

Place one bagel half, cut side up into the bottom ring of breakfast sandwich maker. Place Canadian bacon, tomato and provolone cheese on top.

Lower the cooking plate and top ring; crack an egg into the egg plate and pierce to break the yolk. Sprinkle a few drops of Tabasco (to taste) on top. Top with other bagel half.

Close the cover and cook for 4 to 5 minutes

or until egg is cooked through. Gently slide
the egg plate out and remove sandwich with
a rubber spatula.

Prep time: 4 minutes   Serves: 1

Peach Coconut Cream Croissant

1 small croissant, sliced in half

1 Tbsp. cream cheese

1 Tbsp. peach jam

3 – 4 fresh peach slices

Shredded coconut

Dash of cinnamon and nutmeg

Spread cream cheese and peach jam on both halves of croissant. Place one half in the bottom of breakfast sandwich maker, jam side up. Place peach slices on top. Sprinkle with some shredded coconut and a dash of cinnamon and nutmeg.

Lower cooking plate and top ring. Place other half of croissant on top and close the sandwich maker lid. Cook for 2 – 3 minutes or until the croissant is warmed through.

Carefully remove from sandwich maker and enjoy!

Prep time: 3 minutes   Serves: 1

Veggie Pepper Jack Sandwich with Arugula

1 multigrain English muffin, split

Sliced onion, bell pepper and radish

A few arugula leaves

1 slice Pepper Jack cheese

1 egg

Place one English muffin half, cut side up into the bottom ring of breakfast sandwich maker. Place slices of onion, bell pepper, radish, arugula leaves and Pepper Jack cheese on top.

Lower the cooking plate and top ring; crack an egg into the egg plate and pierce to break the yolk. Top with other muffin half.

Close the cover and cook for 4 to 5 minutes or until egg is cooked through. Gently slide the egg plate out and remove sandwich with

a rubber spatula.

Prep time: 4 minutes   Serves: 1

Bacon & Green Chili Croissant

1 medium croissant, sliced in half

2 tsp. mayonnaise

2 slices bacon

1 slice fresh tomato

1 – 2 tsp. canned diced green chilis

1 slice Swiss cheese

Dash of chili powder

1 egg

Spread mayonnaise on both halves of croissant. Place one half in the bottom of your breakfast sandwich maker, mayo side up. Place bacon, tomato, green chili and Swiss cheese on top. Sprinkle with a dash of chili powder.

Lower cooking plate and top ring. Crack an

egg into the egg plate, piercing the yolk to break it. Top with other croissant half and cook for 4 – 5 minutes, or until egg is cooked through.

Gently slide the egg plate out and carefully remove sandwich with a rubber spatula.

Prep time: 5 minutes   Serves: 1

Sausage & Gravy Biscuit

1 store bought or homemade biscuit, sliced in half

1 – 2 Tbsp. store bought country gravy

1 precooked sausage patty

1 slice cheddar cheese

1 egg

Spread the country gravy on both biscuit halves. Place one biscuit half, cut side up into the bottom ring of breakfast sandwich maker. Place sausage patty and cheddar cheese on top.

Lower the cooking plate and top ring; crack an egg into the egg plate and pierce to break the yolk. Top with other biscuit half.

Close the cover and cook for 4 to 5 minutes or until egg is cooked through. Gently slide the egg plate out and remove sandwich with

a rubber spatula.

Prep time: 4 minutes   **Serves: 1**

Tomato-Basil with Mozzarella Sandwich

2 slices specialty bread such as focaccia or sour dough

2 slices tomato

A few fresh basil leaves

1 – 2 slices fresh mozzarella

A few drops of balsamic vinegar

1 egg

Sea salt and pepper

Place one slice of bread into the bottom ring of breakfast sandwich maker. Place tomatoes, basil and mozzarella cheese on top. Sprinkle with balsamic vinegar.

Lower the cooking plate and top ring; crack an egg into the egg plate and pierce to break the yolk. Sprinkle with sea salt and pepper and top with other slice of bread.

Close the cover and cook for 4 to 5 minutes or until egg is cooked through. Gently slide the egg plate out and remove sandwich with a rubber spatula. Slice in half and enjoy!

Prep time: 5 minutes   Serves: 1

Caramel Cashew Waffle Sandwich

2 small round waffles (store bought or homemade)

1 Tbsp. store bought caramel sauce

2 Tbsp. finely chopped cashews

2 strips bacon

1 egg

Spread caramel sauce on both waffles. Place one waffle into the bottom ring of breakfast sandwich maker, caramel side up. Sprinkle cashews on top, then top with bacon.

Lower the cooking plate and top ring; crack an egg into the egg plate and pierce to break the yolk. Top with other waffle.

Close the cover and cook for 4 to 5 minutes or until egg is cooked through. Gently slide

the egg plate out and remove sandwich with
a rubber spatula and slice in half.

Prep time: 3 minutes   Serves: 1

Greek Cucumber-Yogurt Flatbread

2 slices flatbread

1 Tbsp. plain yogurt

1 slice tomato

Cucumber slices

Feta cheese

Fresh chopped parsley

1 Tbsp. milk

1 egg

Sea salt and pepper

Spread yogurt on both slices of flatbread. Place one slice into the bottom ring of breakfast sandwich maker, yogurt side up. Place tomato, cucumber slices, feta cheese and some fresh parsley on top.

In a small bowl, whisk together milk, egg, sea

salt and pepper. Lower the cooking plate and top ring; pour egg mixture into the egg plate. Top with other piece of flatbread.

Close the cover and cook for 4 to 5 minutes. Slide the egg plate out and remove sandwich with a rubber spatula.

Prep time: 5 minutes   Serves: 1

Monte-Cristo with a Twist

2 slices French or sour dough bread

Butter

Grape jelly

1 slice ham

1 slice provolone cheese

1 egg

Powdered sugar

Butter the outside of each slice of bread.
Spread grape jelly on the inside of both
slices. Place one slice into the bottom ring of
breakfast sandwich maker, jelly side up.
Place ham and provolone cheese on top.

Lower the cooking plate and top ring; crack
an egg into the egg plate and pierce to break
the yolk. Top with other slice of bread.

Close the cover and cook for 4 to 5 minutes
or until egg is cooked through. Gently slide
the egg plate out and remove sandwich with
a rubber spatula. Dust with powdered sugar
and serve.

Prep time: 3 minutes   Serves: 1

Orange Dream Donut

1 medium glazed donut, sliced in half
lengthwise

Cream cheese

Orange marmalade

1 tsp. orange zest

1 egg

Sea salt and pepper

Spread cream cheese and orange marmalade
on both donut halves. Place one half into the
bottom ring of breakfast sandwich maker,
jam side up. Sprinkle with orange zest.

Lower the cooking plate and top ring; crack
an egg into the egg plate and pierce to break
the yolk; sprinkle with sea salt and pepper.
Top with other donut half.

Close the cover and cook for 4 to 5 minutes

or until egg is cooked through. Gently slide the egg plate out and remove donut with a rubber spatula.

Prep time: 5 minutes   Serves: 1

Turkey Bacon and Cranberry Biscuit

1 store bought or homemade biscuit, sliced in half

1 Tbsp. canned cranberry sauce

2 slices turkey bacon

1 slice Swiss cheese

1 egg

Spread cranberry sauce on both biscuit halves. Place one half into the bottom ring of breakfast sandwich maker, cranberry side up. Place turkey bacon and Swiss cheese on top.

Lower the cooking plate and top ring; crack an egg into the egg plate and pierce to break the yolk. Top with other biscuit half.

Close the cover and cook for 4 to 5 minutes

or until egg is cooked through. Gently slide
the egg plate out and remove sandwich with
a rubber spatula.

Prep time: 4 minutes   Serves: 1

Ultimate BLT Melt

1 multigrain English muffin, split

1 Tbsp. mayonnaise

1 slice tomato

2 slices smoked bacon

$^1/_2$ slice cheddar cheese

$^1/_2$ slice Monterey Jack cheese

Baby spinach leaves

1 Tbsp. milk

1 egg

1 Tbsp. diced onion

1 tsp. diced jalapeño

Sea salt and pepper

Spread mayonnaise on both English muffin halves. Place one half into the bottom ring of

breakfast sandwich maker, mayo side up.
Place tomato, bacon, cheddar cheese,
Monterey Jack cheese and spinach leaves on
top.

In a small bowl, whisk together milk, egg,
onion, jalapeño, sea salt and pepper. Lower
the cooking plate and top ring; pour in egg
mixture. Top with other muffin half.

Close the cover and cook for 4 to 5 minutes
or until egg is cooked through and cheeses
are melted. Gently slide the egg plate out and
remove sandwich with a rubber spatula.

Prep time: 8 minutes   Serves: 1

Basil-Strawberry Walnut Sandwich

1 store bought or homemade biscuit, split

2 fresh strawberries, slices

1 Tbsp. finely chopped walnuts

Basil leaves

1 slice gruyere cheese

1 egg

Place one biscuit half into the bottom ring of breakfast sandwich maker. Place sliced strawberries, walnuts, a few basil leaves and gruyere cheese on top.

Lower the cooking plate and top ring; crack an egg into the egg plate and pierce to break the yolk. Top with other biscuit half.

Close the cover and cook for 4 to 5 minutes or until egg is cooked through. Gently slide

the egg plate out, remove sandwich with a
rubber spatula and enjoy!

Prep time: 5 minutes   Serves: 1

Choco-Coconut Nut Quesadilla

2 small corn tortillas

2 tsp. chocolate hazelnut spread

2 tsp. almond butter

Shredded coconut

Honey or agave nectar

Cinnamon

Spread chocolate hazelnut spread and almond butter on both tortillas. Place one tortilla into the bottom ring of breakfast sandwich maker, nut butter side up. Sprinkle with coconut, drizzle with honey or agave and add a dash of cinnamon. Cover with other tortilla

Close the cover and cook for 3 to 4 minutes or until warmed through. Gently remove with a rubber spatula. Slice in half or roll up.

Prep time: 3 minutes   Serves: 1

Creamy Strawberry Mint Croissant

1 small croissant, sliced in half

1 Tbsp. cream cheese

1 Tbsp. strawberry jam

1 – 2 fresh strawberries, sliced

A few fresh mint leaves

Spread cream cheese and strawberry jam on both halves of croissant. Place one half in the bottom of breakfast sandwich maker, jam side up. Place strawberry slices on top, followed by a few fresh mint leaves.

Lower the cooking plate and top ring. Place other half of croissant on top and close the sandwich maker lid. Cook for 2 – 3 minutes or until the croissant is warmed through. Carefully remove from sandwich maker.

Prep time: 3 minutes   Serves: 1

Meat Lovers Sandwich

2 slices flatbread

1 tsp. Dijon mustard

1 slice ham

2 slices bacon

1 precooked sausage patty

1 slice smoked Gouda cheese

1 egg

Sea salt and pepper

Spread Dijon mustard on both flatbread slices. Place one slice into the bottom ring of breakfast sandwich maker, mustard side up. Place ham, bacon, sausage and Gouda cheese on top.

Lower the cooking plate and top ring; crack an egg into the egg plate and pierce to break the yolk. Season with sea salt and pepper and top with other piece of flatbread.

Close the cover and cook for 4 to 5 minutes or until egg is cooked through. Gently slide the egg plate out and remove sandwich with a rubber spatula.

Prep time: 5 minutes   Serves: 1

Mexican Salsa Sandwich

2 slices Texas toast

2 Tbsp. diced tomatoes

1 Tbsp. diced onion

1 Tbsp. diced bell pepper

1 Tbsp. finely chopped cilantro

Dash of sugar

Dash of white vinegar

Juice from 1 lime

Sea salt and pepper

1 slice Monterey Jack cheese

1 egg

In a small bowl combine tomatoes, onion, bell pepper, cilantro, sugar, white vinegar, lime juice, sea salt and pepper; mix well.

Spread on one half of Texas toast and place into the bottom ring of sandwich maker. Top with Monterey Jack cheese.

Lower the cooking plate and top ring; crack an egg into the egg plate and pierce to break the yolk. Top with other slice of Texas toast.

Close the cover and cook for 4 to 5 minutes or until egg is cooked through. Gently slide the egg plate out and remove sandwich with a rubber spatula.

Prep time: 10 minutes   Serves: 1

Peach Basil Croissant

1 small croissant, sliced in half

1 – 2 Tbsp. cottage cheese

2 tsp. peach jam

Fresh sliced peaches

Basil leaves

Dash of cinnamon

Spread cottage cheese and peach jam on both croissant halves. Place one half into the bottom ring of breakfast sandwich maker, jam side up. Place peach slices and basil leaves on top. Sprinkle with cinnamon.

Lower the cooking plate and top ring; top with other croissant half. Close the cover and cook for 3 to 4 minutes or until sandwich is warmed through. Remove from sandwich maker and enjoy!

Prep time: 4 minutes   Serves: 1

Piña Colada Croissant

1 small croissant, sliced in half

1 Tbsp. cream cheese

1 – 2 Tbsp. finely chopped pineapple

Shredded coconut

Honey

Spread cream cheese on both croissant halves. Place one half into the bottom ring of breakfast sandwich maker, cut side up. Place chopped pineapple and shredded coconut on top. Drizzle with honey.

Lower the cooking plate and top ring; top with other croissant half. Close the cover and cook for 3 to 4 minutes or until sandwich is warmed through. Open sandwich maker and remove sandwich.

Prep time: 4 minutes   Serves: 1

Beans & Veggies Sandwich

2 slices multigrain bread

2 Tbsp. canned black beans

2 tsp. diced green onion

2 tsp. shredded carrot

2 tsp. shredded radish

1 slice Pepper Jack cheese

1 egg

Sea salt and pepper

Spread black beans on both slices of bread. Place one slice, beans side up, into the bottom ring of sandwich maker. Sprinkle green onion, carrot and radish on top. Top with Pepper Jack cheese.

Lower the cooking plate and top ring; crack an egg into the egg plate and pierce to break the yolk. Season with sea salt and pepper.

58

Top with other slice of bread.

Close the cover and cook for 4 to 5 minutes or until egg is cooked through. Gently slide the egg plate out and remove sandwich with a rubber spatula.

Prep time: 8 minutes   Serves: 1

Ham-Mango Croissant

1 small croissant, sliced in half

1 slice ham

A few slices mango

Dash of cayenne pepper

1 slice white cheddar cheese

1 egg

Sea salt and pepper

Place one croissant half into the bottom ring of breakfast sandwich maker, cut side up. Place ham and mango on top, and lightly sprinkle with cayenne pepper. Next place the cheddar cheese.

Lower the cooking plate and top ring; crack an egg into the egg plate and pierce to break the yolk. Season with sea salt and pepper. Top with other croissant half.

Close the cover and cook for 4 to 5 minutes or until egg is cooked and sandwich is warmed through. Carefully remove sandwich with a rubber spatula.

Prep time: 5 minutes   Serves: 1

Fruit Salad Sandwich with Lemon

1 store bought or homemade biscuit

1 Tbsp. strawberry flavored cream cheese

A few slices of banana, apple, grapes, peaches, or any fruit of choice

1 tsp. fresh lemon juice

Chopped mint leaves

Spread cream cheese on both biscuit halves. Place one half into the bottom ring of breakfast sandwich maker, cut side up. Place sliced fruit, drizzle with lemon juice and sprinkle chopped mint leaves over all.

Lower the cooking plate and top ring; top with other biscuit half. Close the cover and cook for 3 to 4 minutes or until sandwich is warmed through. Open sandwich maker, remove sandwich carefully and enjoy!

Prep time: 6 minutes   Serves: 1

Ham and Relish Melt

2 slices white or multigrain bread

Butter

1 Tbsp. sweet pickle relish

1 slice ham

1 slice cheddar cheese

1 egg

Sea salt and pepper

Butter the outside of each slice of bread. Spread relish on the inside of each slice. Place one slice into the bottom ring of breakfast sandwich maker, relish side up. Place ham and cheddar cheese on top.

Lower the cooking plate and top ring; crack an egg into the egg plate and pierce to break the yolk. Season with sea salt and pepper. Top with other slice of bread.

Close the cover and cook for 4 to 5 minutes or until egg is cooked and cheese is melted. Carefully remove sandwich with a rubber spatula.

Prep time: 5 minutes   Serves: 1

Thai Breakfast Sandwich

2 slices whole wheat bread

1 Tbsp. peanut butter

1 Tbsp. shredded carrots

1 Tbsp. bean sprouts

1 tsp. finely chopped cilantro

Dash of lime juice

Dash of soy sauce

1 Tbsp. milk

1 egg

Sea salt and pepper

Spread peanut butter on both slices of bread. Place one slice into the bottom ring of breakfast sandwich maker, peanut butter side up. Pile the carrots, bean sprouts and cilantro on top. Sprinkle with lime juice and soy sauce.

In a small bowl whisk together milk, egg, sea salt and pepper. Lower the cooking plate and top ring; pour egg mixture in. Top with other slice of bread.

Close the cover and cook for 4 to 5 minutes or until egg is cooked. Remove sandwich with a rubber spatula.

Prep time: 6 minutes   Serves: 1

Steak & Eggs Sandwich

1 English muffin, split

1 – 2 tsp. creamy horseradish

Thin strips of precooked steak

A few fresh onion rings

1 slice smoked Gouda cheese

1 egg

Sea salt and pepper

Spread the horseradish on both English muffin halves. Place one half into the bottom ring of breakfast sandwich maker, cut side up. Place steak, onion and Gouda cheese on top.

Lower the cooking plate and top ring; crack an egg into the egg plate and pierce to break the yolk. Season with sea salt and pepper. Top with other muffin half.

Close the cover and cook for 4 to 5 minutes or until egg is cooked and cheese is melted. Remove sandwich with a rubber spatula and enjoy!

Prep time: 5 minutes   Serves: 1

Gruyere, Apple and Ham Sandwich

1 Ciabatta roll, sliced in half

1 slice ham

A few apple slices

1 slice gruyere cheese

1 Tbsp. milk

2 tsp. diced onion

1 egg

Sea salt and pepper

Place one Ciabatta roll half into the bottom ring of breakfast sandwich maker. Place ham, apple slices and gruyere cheese on top.

In a small bowl whisk together milk, onion, egg, sea salt and pepper. Lower the cooking plate and top ring; pour egg mixture into egg plate. Top with other roll half.

Close the cover and cook for 4 to 5 minutes or until egg is cooked and cheese is melted. Remove sandwich with a rubber spatula.

Prep time: 5 minutes   Serves: 1

Veggie & Cheese Melt

2 slices sour dough bread

1 tomato slice

1 Tbsp. finely chopped spinach

1 Tbsp. finely diced precooked asparagus

A few fresh onion rings

1 slice white cheddar cheese

1 egg

Sea salt and pepper

Place one slice of sour dough bread into the bottom ring of breakfast sandwich maker. Place tomato, spinach, asparagus, onion and white cheddar cheese on top.

Lower the cooking plate and top ring; crack an egg into the egg plate and pierce to break the yolk. Season with sea salt and pepper.

Top with other slice of bread.

Close the cover and cook for 4 to 5 minutes or until egg is cooked and cheese is melted. Carefully remove sandwich with a rubber spatula.

Prep time: 5 minutes   Serves: 1

Blueberry Waffle Sandwich

2 small store bought frozen blueberry waffles

Butter

2 strips bacon

1 slice cheddar cheese

1 egg

Sea salt and pepper

Spread butter on both waffles. Place one into the bottom ring of breakfast sandwich maker, butter side down. Place bacon and cheddar cheese on top.

Lower the cooking plate and top ring; crack an egg into the egg plate and pierce to break the yolk. Season with sea salt and pepper. Top with other waffle.

Close the cover and cook for 4 to 5 minutes or until egg is cooked and cheese is melted.

Remove sandwich with a rubber spatula.

Prep time: 5 minutes   Serves: 1

Hash Browns & Sausage Sandwich

2 slices multigrain bread

1 Tbsp. butter

1 cup frozen hash browns

1 precooked sausage patty

1 slice provolone cheese

1 egg

In a small skillet heat the butter over medium heat. Place hash browns over the butter in a single layer and let fry for about 5 minutes or until a brown crust forms on the bottom.

Place one slice of bread into the bottom ring of breakfast sandwich maker. Top with hash browns, sausage and provolone cheese.

Lower the cooking plate and top ring; crack

an egg into the egg plate and pierce to break the yolk. Top with other slice of bread.

Close the cover and cook for 4 to 5 minutes or until egg is cooked. Slide the egg plate out, remove sandwich with a rubber spatula and enjoy!

Prep time: 10 minutes   Serves: 1

Portabella Havarti Melt

2 slices crusty white bread

2 tsp. mayonnaise

1 tsp. Dijon mustard

1 portabella mushroom cap

Spinach leaves

1 slice dill havarti cheese

1 egg

Spread mayonnaise and Dijon mustard on both slices of bread. Place one slice, mayo side up into the bottom ring of breakfast sandwich maker. Place portabella mushroom, spinach leaves and havarti cheese on top.

Lower the cooking plate and top ring; crack an egg into the egg plate and pierce to break the yolk. Top with other slice of bread.

Close the cover and cook for 4 to 5 minutes or until egg is cooked through. Gently slide the egg plate out and remove sandwich with a rubber spatula.

Prep time: 4 minutes   Serves: 1

Chocolate Chip Waffle Sandwich

2 small frozen waffles

1 Tbsp. cream cheese

1 Tbsp. mini chocolate chips

1 Tbsp. milk

1 egg

Sea salt and pepper

Spread cream cheese on both waffles. Place one, cream cheese side up into the bottom ring of breakfast sandwich maker. Place chocolate chips on top.

In a small bowl, whisk together milk, egg, sea salt and pepper. Lower the cooking plate and top ring; pour egg mixture into egg plate. Top with other waffle.

Close the cover and cook for 4 to 5 minutes or until egg is cooked through. Gently slide

the egg plate out, remove sandwich with a rubber spatula and enjoy!

Prep time: 5 minutes   Serves: 1

Chicken, Avocado and Swiss Croissant

1 small croissant, sliced in half

1 Tbsp. herb and chive cream cheese

Strips of precooked chicken breast

Avocado slices

Sea salt and pepper

1 slice Swiss cheese

1 egg

Spread the cream cheese on both halves of croissant. Place one half, cut side up into the bottom ring of breakfast sandwich maker. Place chicken breast and avocado on top; sprinkle with sea salt and pepper. Top with Swiss cheese.

Lower the cooking plate and top ring; crack the egg into the egg plate and pierce to break the yolk. Top with other croissant half.

Close the cover and cook for 4 to 5 minutes or until egg is cooked through. Slide the egg plate out by turning clockwise and remove sandwich with a rubber spatula.

Prep time: 5 minutes   Serves: 1

Breakfast Pizza Sandwich

2 pieces pita bread, cut to fit sandwich maker

2 Tbsp. store bought marinara sauce

1 slice ham

A few slices of pepperoni

Basil leaves

1 – 2 slices mozzarella cheese

1 egg

Spread marinara sauce on both pieces of pita bread. Place one piece into the bottom ring of breakfast sandwich maker, marinara side up. Place ham, pepperoni, basil and mozzarella cheese on top.

Lower the cooking plate and top ring; crack an egg into the egg plate and pierce to break the yolk. Top with other piece of pita bread.

Close the cover and cook for 4 to 5 minutes or until egg is cooked through. Gently slide the egg plate out, remove sandwich with a rubber spatula and enjoy!

Prep time: 5 minutes   Serves: 1

Creamy Brie & Fruit Sandwich

2 slices crusty white bread, crusts removed

1 – 2 Tbsp. soft brie cheese

2 strawberries, sliced

3 – 4 grapes, sliced

A few blueberries

1 Tbsp. finely chopped pecans

Honey

Spread brie cheese on both bread slices.
Place one slice into the bottom ring of
breakfast sandwich maker, brie side up.
Place sliced strawberries, grapes, blueberries
and chopped pecans on top. Drizzle with
honey.

Lower the cooking plate and top ring; top
with other slice of bread. Close the cover and
cook for 3 to 4 minutes or until sandwich is

warm and cheese is melted. Remove
sandwich with a rubber spatula and enjoy!

Prep time: 5 minutes   Serves: 1

Mediterranean Croissant

1 small croissant, sliced in half

1 Tbsp. store bought pesto

1 Tbsp. sun-dried tomatoes

Baby spinach leaves

1 slice havarti cheese

1 egg

Spread pesto on both croissant halves. Place one half into the bottom ring of breakfast sandwich maker, pesto side up. Place sun-dried tomatoes, a few spinach leaves and havarti cheese on top.

Lower the cooking plate and top ring; crack an egg into the egg plate and pierce to break the yolk. Top with other croissant half.

Close the cover and cook for 4 to 5 minutes or until egg is cooked through and cheese is melted. Gently slide the egg plate out and remove sandwich with a rubber spatula.

Prep time: 5 minutes   Serves: 1

Lox and Capers Breakfast Bagel

1 multigrain bagel, split

1 Tbsp. cream cheese

2 – 3 oz. lox (smoked salmon)

Cucumber slices

Red onion slices

1 $\frac{1}{2}$ tsp. capers

1 egg

Spread cream cheese on both bagel halves. Place one half into the bottom ring of breakfast sandwich maker, cream cheese side up. Place smoked salmon, cucumber slices, red onion slices and capers on top.

Lower the cooking plate and top ring; crack an egg into the egg plate and pierce to break the yolk. Top with other bagel half.

Close the cover and cook for 4 to 5 minutes or until egg is cooked. Gently slide the egg plate out. Remove sandwich with a rubber spatula and enjoy!

Prep time: 5 minutes   Serves: 1

Avocado Mash Sandwich

2 slices French bread

$^1/_2$ small avocado

1 Tbsp. diced tomato

$^1/_4$ tsp. garlic salt

Black pepper

1 slice provolone cheese

1 egg

Place one slice of French bread into the bottom ring of breakfast sandwich maker. In a small bowl, mash together avocado, tomato, garlic salt and pepper using a fork. Place avocado mixture on French bread slice and top with provolone cheese.

Lower the cooking plate and top ring; crack an egg into the egg plate and pierce to break the yolk. Top with other slice of French bread.

Close the cover and cook for 4 to 5 minutes or until egg is cooked through. Gently slide the egg plate out and remove sandwich with a rubber spatula.

Prep time: 8 minutes   Serves: 1

Chocolate Hazelnut Croissant with Blueberries and Raspberries

1 small croissant, sliced in half

1 Tbsp. chocolate hazelnut spread

1 Tbsp. crushed hazelnuts

A few fresh blueberries and raspberries

Spread chocolate hazelnut spread on bottom half of croissant. Place in the bottom of breakfast sandwich maker. Sprinkle with hazelnuts and berries.

Lower the cooking plate and top ring. Place other half of croissant on top and close the sandwich maker lid. Cook for 2 – 3 minutes or until croissant is warm. Carefully remove from sandwich maker and enjoy!

Prep time: 4 minutes   Serves: 1

Pear & Greens Sandwich

1 biscuit, split

1 Tbsp. ricotta cheese

Pear slices

Piece of butter lettuce

1 Tbsp. finely chopped walnuts

Spread ricotta cheese on both biscuit halves. Place one half into the bottom ring of breakfast sandwich maker, cheese side up. Place pear slices, butter lettuce and walnuts on top.

Lower the cooking plate and top ring; top with other biscuit half. Close the cover and cook for 3 to 4 minutes or until sandwich is warm. Remove with a rubber spatula and enjoy!

Prep time: 5 minutes   Serves: 1

Mushroom & Swiss Bagel

1 multigrain bagel, split

2 large mushrooms, sliced

1 tsp. butter

Sea salt and pepper

1 slice Swiss cheese

1 egg

Place one bagel half, cut side up into the bottom ring of breakfast sandwich maker.

In a small skillet over medium heat, sauté mushrooms in butter until they shrink and begin to let out moisture. Season with sea salt and pepper. Place mushrooms on top of bagel and cover with Swiss cheese.

Lower the cooking plate and top ring; crack an egg into the egg plate and pierce to break the yolk. Top with other bagel half.

Close the cover and cook for 4 to 5 minutes or until egg is cooked through. Gently slide the egg plate out and remove sandwich with a rubber spatula.

Prep time: 10 minutes   Serves: 1

Thank you for enjoying this cookbook!

About the Author

Mandy Stephens is a busy mom who loves food (especially breakfast!), and has a great time taking care of her husband and kids. She learned to cook as a child and has loved it ever since. She has enjoyed developing recipes that are healthy, yet quick and easy for the busy person.